# BELONGINGS

**David Constantine** was born in 1944 in Salford, Lancashire. He read Modern Languages at Wadham College, Oxford, and lectured in German at Durham from 1969 to 1981 and at Oxford from 1981 to 2000. He is a freelance writer and translator, a Fellow of the Queen's College, Oxford, and was co-editor of *Modern Poetry in Translation* from 2004 to 2013. He lives in Oxford and on Scilly.

He has published eleven books of poetry, five translations and a novel with Bloodaxe. His poetry titles include *Something for the Ghosts* (2002), which was shortlisted for the Whitbread Poetry Award; *Collected Poems* (2004), a Poetry Book Society Recommendation; *Nine Fathom Deep* (2009), *Elder* (2014) and *Belongings* (2020). His Bloodaxe translations include editions of Henri Michaux and Philippe Jaccottet; his *Selected Poems* of Hölderlin, winner of the European Poetry Translation Prize, and his version of *Hölderlin's Sophocles*, combined in a new expanded Hölderlin edition, *Selected Poetry* (2018); and his translation of Hans Magnus Enzensberger's *Lighter Than Air*, winner of the Corneliu M. Popescu Prize for European Poetry Translation. His other books include *A Living Language: Newcastle/Bloodaxe Poetry Lectures* (2004), his translation of Goethe's *Faust* in Penguin Classics (2005, 2009), his monograph, *Poetry* (2013), in Oxford University Press's series *The Literary Agenda*, and his co-translation (with Tom Kuhn) of *The Collected Poems of Bertolt Brecht* (W.W. Norton, 2018).

He has published six collections of short stories, and won the Frank O'Connor International Short Story Award in 2013 for his collection *Tea at the Midland* (Comma Press), and was the first English writer to win this prestigious international fiction award. Four other short story collections, *Under the Dam* (2005), *The Shieling* (2009), *In Another Country: Selected Stories* (2015) and *The Dressing-Up Box* (2019), and his second novel, *The Life-Writer* (2015), are published by Comma Press. His story 'Tea at the Midland' won the BBC National Short Story Award in 2010, while 'In Another Country' was adapted into *45 Years*, a major film starring Tom Courtney and Charlotte Rampling.

# DAVID CONSTANTINE

# Belongings

BLOODAXE BOOKS

ISBN: 978 1 78037 520 5

First published 2020 by
Bloodaxe Books Ltd,
Eastburn,
South Park,
Hexham,
Northumberland NE46 1BS.

www.bloodaxebooks.com
For further information about Bloodaxe titles
please visit our website and join our mailing list
or write to the above address for a catalogue

Supported using public funding by
**ARTS COUNCIL
ENGLAND**

Cover design: Neil Astley & Pamela Robertson-Pearce.

Printed in Great Britain by Bell & Bain Limited, Glasgow, Scotland, on
acid-free paper sourced from mills with FSC chain of custody certification.

# ACKNOWLEDGEMENTS

Acknowledgements and thanks are due to the editors of the following magazines and anthologies in which some of these poems first appeared: *Bracken*, *Hands & Wings* (White Rat Press), *more raw material* (Lucifer Press), *Ten Poems about Walking* (Candlestick Press), *Ploughshares*, *Poetry London*, *Poetry Salzburg*, *The Long White Thread of Words* (Smokestack Books), *The North*, *The Reader* and *St Anne's Review*. The Poetry Business published a substantial selection in *For the Love of it* (2018).

'Ballad of the barge from hell', 'Ballad of the slave ship in the eye of heaven' and 'Song: The way things are is the way things have to be' are from plays of mine broadcast on BBC Radio 3, the first two from *The Good Ship Esperanza*, the third from *The Tidebreak*.

# CONTENTS

1

# My recent encounter with the Good Angel

### 1

The Good Angel led me up the ridge of a high mountain and at the summit she halted.

### 2

It was an ordinary working day she had fetched me out of.

### 3

See there, she said.

### 4

For once the view was clear in every direction and I turned as she turned and saw all that she was offering me.

### 5

I'm not offering you anything, she said.

### 6

I saw all that with the open palm of her right hand she was showing me as she turned and I turned with her through the degrees of the four quarters of the compass.

### 7

You see a very small portion of one zone of a smidgen of the whole earth which is itself, from any reasonable perspective, no larger than the smallest imaginable grain of sand, she said.

### 8

I answered her that to broach even the smallest portion of what she had shown me I should need nine lives not one.

### 9

That's true, she said.

**10**

And of your one, she added, of its three score years and ten, sixty-nine will not come again.

**11**

West the sea shone.

**12**

North, east and south were mountains, hills, valleys, rivers, streams and small climbing and winding roads and paths.

**13**

The terrain was intricately infolded and my vision felt for me in among the curving possibilities.

**14**

I felt how they pushed in, forked, opened, ramified ever more finely climbing.

**15**

I saw ways of exploration without paths.

**16**

For the lie of the land itself, its own suggestions, its bidding and encouragement would suffice.

**17**

From where we stood, the ridge put out long feelers, outriders of itself which only very gradually declined into the valleys.

**18**

Yes, said the Angel, long highways.

**19**

And I can tell you for a fact, she added, that the views would shift significantly step by step, yard by yard, furlong by furlong, as you proceeded.

**20**

And I suppose you might lie somewhere in the heather or the blonde grass on one or another limb of any of these many visible mountain backs and watch the sky inch peaceably towards nightfall.

**21**

I might, I said.

**22**

Indeed I might.

**23**

Also to be seen were human dwellings, some quite isolated, others gathered together in villages.

**24**

Or, she continued, when you had steeped yourself enough in solitude, when you felt like it, in your own good time, you might slither down to a pub, drink quickly, eat voraciously and torkel on a little way to some safe hiding place and pass over into sleep listening to the owls.

**25**

And wake hearing the cuckoo.

**26**

The sky was very lightly veiled.

**27**

Everything lay before me as though for my contemplation.

**28**

And as though in that contemplation I might collect myself into a state of body and soul in which my life would thrive as never before.

**29**

It would thrive by knowing the good earth better, loving her more thoroughly.

**30**

But I saw too much, desired too much, and a voice I knew to be the Devil's said: Too late.

**31**

Don't be glum, said the Good Angel, I'm no expert but I shouldn't think next year would be your last.

**32**

In these parts at least, life expectancy among humans has increased since the days of the Preacher.

**33**

And you kept up with me pretty well on the climb.

## Red

On my geological map of Manchester
The drift edition of 1949
Most is washed over in a faint blue or a faint pink
For the boulder clay and the glacial sand and gravel

Travelled down from the Lake District. Also
Much faded sepia, for the alluvial terraces
Along our soiled river. I wanted outcrops, faces
Daylight apparitions of the city's bedrock

And it took a while of poring till I found a small
Dull smear denoting Bunter Sandstone. Then I walked fast
To the locus itself, a railway cutting
Behind the hospital I was born in. Stood looking:

Nothing bright about it. It was soot black. Touched it:
Black on my fingers. Still I believed in it, the red
From the era of the Greatest Extinction. Yes
After my fashion I saw the bright red in there

Waiting. And I believe it was that moment
Of a boy staring for the red stone through the soot
In a railway cutting close to home that drove me
Again and again to the uplands between the conurbations

The White Peak and the Dark
On paths as many as those that criss-cross your palms
Or climb the *arbor vitae* in your head
Or to all your body's provinces feed the blood.

# Lake

Sole self that day with a working pair of legs
A beating heart, attentive senses, climbed
High enough, far away enough, slowly
Against the river's hurry, quietly

Against the din of it, keeping close to it
And passing the highest shieling that an ash
Had burst as thinking will a head, I came
At dusk to a lake in its own terrain.

There the hills backed off in a spacious horseshoe
On that flat plane I was the only upright
The banks were low, looped in a contour line
The lake had nothing to mirror but the sky.

Sole self I bedded down close as I could
To listen: lapping, birdlife homing, settling
I watched the wind shunting the low black clouds
In tatters, fast, under a pale still ceiling.

Woke once or twice feeling a breath of rain
Glimpsed, silver on black, bits of a star-figure
Heard very high a flight of fellow humans
Touching on dawn after the black Atlantic.

**Puddles on the track...**


Puddles on the track and a man striding along
Up here in the sun he strides among these dazzling waters
Between earth and heaven, the silver brief appearances

Exhaling into thin air... Biped, lucky human
No wonder he exults: on his left hand far below him
He has the same willing element, water, a slim

And sinuous deep body of her lying
Shaped by a contour in a semblance of stillness, she
The discloser of any terrain's true self

To the sun and stars... This fortunate
Sentient remembering imagining man-child
Up here striding among the liquid bright appearances

Brief as will-o'-the-wisps, rainbows, damsel flies
Easily he can recall himself and foresee himself again as
The pale naked swimmer to the centre of such a lake

Idling there like a compass needle on her surface tension
On a thin stratum of warmth and seeing his bloodways
In the shut eyelids... O water, sweet water

Tippling rain, seeker-out of gradients
White torrents down the creases of every declivity
Into the waiting hollows, you have never settled for less

Than the maximum possible plenitude of which
Over the lip of it, you murmur... A while yet
He wants to be allowed his life on earth as an agile psyche

Booted, striding in sunlight on a high track
Among the vanishing puddles and below him, your lover
A lake of you on his left hand, outliving him

# Maps

Thanks be to the map-makers that they have devised
Signs, a whole system, intelligible to all comers
To denote what's locally there. Leave the B road
At a level crossing, head north, enter a mixed wood

Catch hold of its stream and in less than a mile
You will emerge on a steepening slope. Outcrop
Scree, a small lake... Thank them for that
But more still for the space they let you into

Through every pictogram. Two hundred miles away
You can tell whether the church in question
Has a tower, a spire or neither, but not
Whether listening to the sermon you'd have been distracted

By mermaids and green men. Behind the sign
Into the vacancy, oh the inrush of presence
The holy particulars! The map-makers have represented
Some of the many incarnations of water

But not my drying your chilled feet in a handkerchief
Nor the licks of salt. Reading the map afterwards
Assures us of our hinterland, all we got by heart
Through our boot-soles from the braille of the terrain

And all that our fingers learned by digging in
And hauling up our bodyweight. There it is
Our route, very public, anyone can follow it
But only the walkers know it for a song-line

With undertones. Thanks be then to the makers
Of agreed markers, conventional signs
Among the current place names. In any company
I can say aloud, Yes, she is my friend.

## How it saddened me...

How it saddened me after one last time
Tracing with a forefinger the remembered route
Into the tightening contours to where, almost contented
We had turned with the wide-open sky behind us
Back down the stream that was becoming its river-self
Down and down in a kind of satisfaction
That we were leaving the immense rest unseen
Slowly with a finger trailing the way into the flatlands
How it dejected me concluding that last after-journey
To fold the map and slot it back where it belongs
In the hoard of the trodden, the untrodden
The never now by us to be trodden paths.

# Eye test

The ophthalmologist asked what could I see.
Dead stuff floating, I replied, the usual wispy debris
And some days a black spot, a tiny black moon
Sidles across the right eye on a trajectory of its own.

I said I liked to lie on hills under big skies
Viewing only the muted red inside my lids.
I can show you better than that, she said. And did:
She showed me the tracery of blood on the globes of the eyes

The paths and streams of it. Her science, her instruments
Gave me a joyous peace of mind. I shall lie
High in the heather under the sun in a still excitement
And shut my eyes and watch the *arbor vitae*

Putting up, putting out through the rings of bone
Ever more finely on the vast and painless red
Branching, leafing, flowering. Happy the dead
Who out of their life's deep humus show what they have seen.

2

# For the love of it

Black hull, two brick-red sails, full tide
Not six o'clock yet on the soft breath of a southerly
Under the clearing sky the first small boat puts out
Down the quiet sound towards the continuous mêlée
Of the whole Atlantic. You know this room

At midsummer very early how the sun slants in
And over the watcher's shoulder flames up silver
In the seahorse looking glass and rising
Angles down across the dark blue length and breadth
Of the waking sleeper's bed. I see them side by side

Standing quiet. They can handle their craft
And read the charts and perhaps the stars and know
The one thing certain about the weather is that it's changeable
And look: red sails, black hull, solely for love
They put out into an ocean, for the risky love of it.

# High wind, sunset, high spring tide

Water-fire, tongued up and whirling
And bodies of water in the appearance of hard turquoise
Slipping into milk, into flocks of snow, a small rain
Ghosts in the look of rainbows and tasting of salt

And the din of it, the sun must roar like that
Out of which it has travelled across an ocean
With the wind behind it, the long fetch
Of the shapes of chaos, the makings, unmakings

None aspiring to another condition, all
Bound for ever in the play of the laws of flux
Which are fine and various, beyond calculation
And immutable. With that savage landfall

For a while I stood level and wrack
Ripped from its tenure was held up heraldic
Tined, branching and fingering on a white crest
For my brief contemplation and in a broken dazzle

Along with stones as rounded as cannonballs came
Flung in also, bloody, a seal pup
And when the blanket of the foam withdrew
There he lay, nosing towards our so-called terra firma

This creature very adept in its given element
Delivered gashed and pumping with hot blood
Into a bay as small as my span of years
That embraces as I do a speck of the possible

Chaos drove, the dance that haunts our blood
And the holes of the eyes and the curious brain took it in
A little, its breath ripped mine from my mouth
And I clutched at straws of our difference

Love, grief

# Full moon and cloud-cover

Up there, walking on the cloud-cover you would cast
A shadow as black and sharp as obsidian. Down here
Through fourteen hours of moon in a softened radiance
Diffused, pearl-silver-grey, your midnight waking
At the uncurtained window viewing the islands
The sisters, the merry maidens, the stone dancers
Within whose broken ring the moon, even occluded
In that arena shows how she plays the sea
You do not forget there exists an upper region
A zone of brilliance, clarity without mercy
Vast, cold, unbreathable, the light, the light, the light
And a covering of cloud between it and our dwellings
A cover any rising wind will tear to shreds.

# Abandoned bulb fields under Samson Hill

This is what it looks like, to be let go
To be released from service into your own sweet time
This carelessness, this abundance
Of paper whites, avalanches, soleils d'or
Let to be what they want under the chamber tombs.

One February after another if you knew what you were looking for
Less and less clearly you could discern the old rows
And mark with satisfaction that vanishing order
As the sign of the multitude coming into their own.

Nobody visits any more with flames to burn off the dead haulms
And force the lives biding tight in the earth out into the daylight early.
Now they store their own inhalation of the sun
And make their appearance when they feel like it.
And the competition on these scraps of land, the brambles
Bracken, gorse, foxgloves, honeysuckle, all that life too
On the same decision of relinquishing
Was let be. Henceforth do as you please! So through the chaos
Of last year's dead – harsh, spikey, encumbering – and this year's
New beginnings, rise now
The useless, the unmarketable, douce and insistent blooms
Earthlings respiring perfume, with no price on their heads.

It is thirty years or more since, after twice that toll
Of struggle, worry, eye on the clock and the weather, the tenants departed
And let the ploughed rows loose into idle beauty.

The walls, all that heaving and fitting under the sun and the moon
All that wrenching granite out of the ground, freeing up the ground
Clearing it of every impediment, to work it, to make it work
All of that done with now and the walls
Still standing that may stand till kingdom come
Look almost like outstretched arms
Ushering delivery, life in freedom, the living waters, grace

Down the slopes and over the toppled gates to the low cliff –
Oh that spill of narcissi to the edge!
You'd think they might advance over the drowned fields and the drowned
        habitations
To the next hill, the next small island
And carry their scented breath up to the neighbours' tumuli.

# Strata

Just below the turf (in its season bright with thrift)
Among the dead tubes of bracken roots in the good black earth they nourish
There's a deposit of grey-white polystyrene
Soft loose leaves crumbling into small granules
Which is its way of living for ever. East of that and lower

Held visible for now in a toppling overhang
There's the disarticulated skeleton of quite a large animal
Dull-orange bones, some say of Bess, the mare Ted's grandfather
Worked these bulb fields with (how the children loved her!)
And here she died and here he buried her. Below that grave

Under the abandoned fields there was a settlement
The sea discovered it, many flints and shards, gone to museums now
Or the sea took them. But today between the tides
Having the warming February sun and the south wind at my back
When I conducted a finger-tip search of the cliff-face

I did light on a flint, not a tool but the faceted flake
And making of one, a thumb-nail thing, and holding it up to the sun
Saw the jagged edge of it translucent. Then
Not even the freed and dancing narcissi were gladder of their lives
Than I was of ours, love, on this scrap of terra firma.

# Landfall

One by one with the swallows and with their grace
And knowledge of the winds, towards evening
The first sails arrive, in silence, slowly, almost shyly
As though abashed by their own entrance out of the ocean
Into the quiet sound. These mariners are familiar.
They moor for the night, next day they come ashore
And walk the only road. In the churchyard
(Just above the tide) they will be noticed searching
For any additions to the stones. Of the swallows
Most are passing, but some on this rock will lodge
And certain households will accommodate again
The gift they have come to feel they could not do without
And often in the black months dared not hope for.
When swallows built their nests in Cleopatra's sails
The augurers shook their heads but any sailor
Making for this first landfall would think it a blessing
To ferry an exhausted migrant along the way.
I watch them from this window over the sound
Hunting, always hunting, they know their purpose.
They have died in abundance, they are not mourned.
The young will carry the knowledge. And now, red sky astern
Another sail leans in. Tomorrow the visitants
Will walk our only road and courteously
Swap news with us of the living and the dead.

# The lucky and the unlucky

### 1

That was the evening the *Grace* appeared
At the mouth of the sound, a brave phenomenon
Blue and orange on the white water
Between the two sheer headlands, nosed around
And leaving then she left our vision opening
Into an Atlantic vacant of humanity.

Northwest, half a hemisphere was quilting over
Flocks, hanks, shreds of woolly softness burning
Chillier than the sea. Those moonless nights
We woke and heard in the hectic breathless zones
The cold and furious serpents of the winds
That circle us all, the lucky and the unlucky.

### 2

That was the afternoon and that the low water.
Wreck there was none. Tomorrow maybe?
Making from shore to point across the weed
My looking intersected with the time of day
The light, the slant on a small pale floor of sand
Where a lifted skirt of wrack had swirled aside.

High-vis, the coastguards rounded the point with staves
And phones looking along the tideline. We enjoyed
A conversation I've enjoyed before:
The wind, the currents, the tide ebbing or flowing...
Some never come up. But warming in my fist:
Faustina; Light-bearing Diana, scried through verdigris.

3

This is the morning, there our little boat
Red and white she rides a jade inrushing sea
Rocks and lifts and seems to fight the mooring
Her partner and exciter in the dance
Among the billion tongues of water-fire
Full in the sun-struck, sun-outflashing race

Of this new day's unstoppable pentecost. Oh swimmer
Lover that you were of solitary moonlight dips
While the *Emerald Dawn* goes through to the fishing grounds
And you are lost and turning still somewhere below her wake
I see the washed-out ghost of you at heaven's window
Pining for Earth, the blue, the lovely-watery.

## Black Dog

Not that I watch for him, but only that when I
Put out the lamp at last it banishes
My strange face from the pane and I see there is
A world, the path, the dunes, the beach, the sea, the sky

And think maybe he'll come, they'll come, that man and his dog
And always first the dog, the quick black spaniel,
A creature innocent of the straight and narrow
Who runs in loops and swerves as though for the fun of it she will

Solve thirteen crazy mazes before breakfast
And wants the Master following her but does not trust
Him to and so keeps circling back
To wind him in for what she wants, that man

Unsmiling, never a civil word
Nor any word at all I've ever heard
But only grunts and mutterings and looking daggers at
Such of his race as still give him good day.

I've never seen her not know where she wants to be
And knowing it she wants him biddable
Down the path to the beach and surf. I watch, I see
She credits him with better than we know.

A while – so long a while! – they're out of sight
Behind the dunes and never, watching, have I not
Lost hope, and never, hopeless, have I got
What hopelessness deserves: to see her never again

The slim black dog, sniffing the salt, heraldic in the bows
Of a small red boat, its daring figurehead
Under a sky ten trillion times her size
A sky piled up most mornings black and red

Gold tumbling though the holes, her in the prow
And Master hunched in the stern steering a course
Past Hangman, Pollack, Hole of the Horse
Out between Gimble and Bad Place, into the open sea.

Lately, that churl, that surly soul, I must confess
That human crouched under his misery
With her, faithful black spaniel, putting out to sea
I have suspected him of happiness.

3

# At the garden centre

On Sundays we go to the garden centre.
Everybody does. We see the same old faces
But nobody says, Weren't you here last week, mate?
It's as if we didn't want to be recognised
At the garden centre on a Sunday. For the men
Being one myself, I've not much sympathy.
Tracksuits are bad but in a bit of warm weather
Sure as death out come the shorts and tee shirts. No
It's the women I feel for, the bearing of children
Can't be easy and the looking after them and still
And for ever and ever the men. If women look that way,
That tired, in my opinion, you can mostly blame the men.
To be honest, I don't much like going to the garden centre
But I don't blame my wife. If anything happened to her
It's pretty certain I'd still be there on Sundays
Trundling a trolley around and not rightly knowing why I'm there.
I see a lot of men at the garden centre lost, like that.
And if what you came for does come back to you
And you look for a member of staff for assistance
As like as not you'll hit on a member of the public:
Sorry, mate, he'll say, I don't work here and to be honest
I was looking for a bit of help myself. Once
I did find a member of staff and I asked him my question
But all he said was, Can't help you there, mate. Sorry.
Everybody's quite matey at the garden centre
But by no means, in my opinion, are the people
On Sundays at the garden centre all that happy.
I think it must be because we shuffle around in trainers
And even if it's in pots and it won't last very long
Everywhere you look there's another form of life
That goes on budding, flowering and fruiting and looking nice
For a while at least. It's then
My heart goes out to the saddened women
Fingering packets of seeds or obviously wondering
Would a little apricot tree survive on any ground they own.

Something forgotten comes into their faces
Not really bearable anymore. And to be fair
I did once see a man in the same condition.
He was wearing the England strip
And holding up a rose in a pot on each big hand
An Iceberg, for all I know, and maybe a Silver Ghost
And he stood there, so to speak, between them
And in tears and when he saw me looking, God
Be my witness, mate, he said, I didn't always look like this.

# The lady on the lid

And in that same tempest the Austrian Ambassador
Fearing he stood on the brink of drowning
Flung his snuff-box, on whose lid was painted
His mistress naked, into the sea. Unlikely
He hoped this would persuade the god Poseidon
To rebuke the wind and the wind would cease
And there'd be a great calm. No, it seems certain
He had no desire to stand in the sodden queue at the Pearly Gates
And be frisked by the thugs of that promoted traitor Peter
And have the lady on his snuff-box lid
Laid in the scales. Poor
Count Anton Franz de Paula Lamberg-Sprinzestein
Ambassador Plenipotentiary to the Court of Ferdinand I
King of the Two Sicilies whom they called 'The Nose'
On board the *Vanguard* in the company
Of Sir William and Lady Hamilton and Rear-Admiral Lord Nelson
Christmas 1798, fleeing the godless French
Arrived alive in Palermo and deciding
It was a false alarm and after all
For the foreseeable future it would be business as usual
He licked the salt from his lips and on the third day
Bought himself a new snuff-box and another lady for the lid.

## My Tilley hat

Tom Stockin, forgive me, I am wearing your Tilley hat.
It blew out of the sea on a storm-force westerly
At Popplestone into a field already sown
With cuttlefish, plastic, pizzles of oar weed, a dead seal
And stones that would break every bone in your body. Your hat
When I ran after it, rose, flew, flopped, rose up again
Like a spent bird. But in the end I nabbed it. Sodden
It was, sodden and smeared, and host to a multitude
Of small worms that had entered through a rip in the crown.
Tom Stockin, till then I never knew I wanted a Tilley hat
But now: How did I manage without? I washed it thoroughly
In soapy water, evicted the beasties, and closed
The head wound with a silver tape. A hat's a hat
They say, and that is that. Unless it's a Tilley hat.
Your name's in the lining, clear, indelibly
With a telephone number half decipherable.
Should I try harder to contact you? I tell myself
You are very likely drowned and what if I got your widow
Or some other loved one? Too distressing. But to be honest
Now that I know I've always wanted a Tilley hat
And the furious January gales have delivered me one
I'm not sure I want you or your descendants
Informed of where it made landfall. I never take it off
Except in the evenings if there's nothing on television
I might study the account of its manufacture and virtues
Printed in English and French over the inner crown
And – bless you for this, Tom – an old love of languages
Revives in me: I see myself at teatime in short trousers
Reading from the HP Sauce bottle to my astonished parents:
This high-quality sauce... Cette sauce de haute qualité...
And now these evenings alone by the driftwood fire
Imagine me, Tom, reading aloud to the lares and penates:
It floats, ties on, repels rain, won't shrink... Il flotte
S'attache, protège contre la pluie, ne rétrécit pas...
I know it by heart, Tom, in the two tongues: le chapeau Tilley

Made in Canada, fait au Canada. I have even wondered
Did you say goodbye to it on your Eastern seaboard, or mid–Atlantic?
Strange things happen. There's a buoy I can see at low water
Through this very window, beached here a century ago
From the Saint Lawrence river. Are you out there, Tom,
Sunk and your Tilley hat floated? Tom Stockin
It is my intention to be cremated in this Tilley hat
And to have my ashes scattered when the wind is easterly
So that if you are indeed lying full fathom five
In a sense you and I may meet and your Tilley hat
After a fashion will be returned to you, Tom Stockin.

## Both knowing, neither saying

We wake, both know, and neither says. Hearing the rain
Knowing you are awake in the dark and listening to the rain
I should not like you to know that I am thinking
Not of the harboured lovers whose contentment
Under the roof is deepened by the wind and the rain
Beneath the cloud, but of a man and woman I have invented
And she has woken alone in a tangled city
Thinking of him who should by now be in the daylight
Above the rain, in the azure, in sunlight thinking
How safe her room will be whose key he has
How close and home her bed will be, this pair
So concentrated in their single longing
Why must I think for him an hour or more of circling
Stacked and queuing in the empyrean and for her
Only confinement under the lowering cloud
And the black rain slanting in the second-circle winds
Into which zone he will at last descend
All hurry by now, all struggle, why can't I
Spare her, my fiction, knots of hopeless panic
Fearing the haste, impatience, anger of the lanes
Trembling in the fear that even such desire as his
Like hers, so clear and sole, will fret itself to death
In all this everyday of thwarting, fury, menace?
Awake, both knowing, neither saying, lying in the dark
Harboured under a roof from the wind and the rain
Why can't I bless even my poor inventions
With easy meetings? Light falling on this cloud
Above gives it the appearance of a soft white bed
And still I lock my lovers in a world of noise
Harsh lighting, error, gridlock, ambulances.

# Recall

That book I borrowed about the lost children
All those years ago, I've had a notification:
They've been going through their records and found it missing
And want it back. I feel ashamed. As you know

I'm a stickler for things like that. I searched high and low
Loft to cellar, shelf after shelf after shelf
Three days and half the nights as well.
Nothing. I even wondered had I left it with you.

Then this morning waking in the dark as usual
I had a sudden live memory of its whereabouts
And crawled in there at once in my dressing gown
And the torch on my forehead. And there it was

I might almost say where it belonged to be
The book with photographs of the lost children. Found
But the state it's in I think they wouldn't thank me
If I did return it. Black and white, you remember

And now every child has faded beyond recovery
Back into the white page, except funnily enough
The lostest of them all, the one we settled on
Because she looked a bit like me and a lot like you

She still hasn't quite gone back wherever they go
When they've been lost too long and nobody will come
And say, You're found, my dearest. I decided
I'd keep this to myself and here I am telling you.

# My neighbour

I had a neighbour once, when his wife left him
He paved over the front garden. Tidier, he said.
If a bit sepulchral, I answered. A year passed
And I saw him on his knees with a lump hammer
Bashing out circles of earth between the slabs.
You be careful, I said. I knew a man in Dukinfield
Lost both eyes doing that. Worse things happen
He said. But nothing did. In the dead of night
I observed him pushing in bulbs the size of cow's eyeballs.
Once a week that winter I asked him was he feeling any better.
No, he answered. I had him in for a Christmas cup of tea.
Then I was away on family-history business. A warm day
In early spring I come up my front garden path
And there he is sitting on a three-legged stool
Among a host of nearly open daffodils.
Triumph of life over death, eh Colin? I said.
He sat there all that day and the next, looking
And on the third day, towards dusk, I saw him rise
And bow his face down and touch with his lips every flower.
Tears obscured my vision, I rummaged for a handkerchief
Saw him appear with the shears and watched him
Behead his beauties one and all. Seeing me on my threshold
Snip, snip, snip, he said. That'll teach her.

# He awoke and found it true

Another thing you don't know and I do
(You never look up, you have no imagination)
High above you there's a woman you can't see from here below.
Admittedly, I can't see her either even though
I often look up and have more than my share of imagination.
A woman – only made of stone, I grant you –
But see her even a split second you'll never be the same again.

She's one of the Seven Deadly Sins and you can guess which one.
And the chap who made her seven hundred years ago
About that sin in particular he knew a thing or two
And the Master said, Alright, alright, Alfie, don't go on and on
Me and the lads'll divvy up the other six and leave her to you
But I'm to tell you His Reverence said if it's you it's on condition
She's round the north end over the cess and out of the public view.

Alf was happy with that. The story goes – and believe me it is true –
That once he'd chosen the stone and got it up there in position
He announced his intention of not coming down again
Until he'd brought her out fit to be looked at by no one
But himself and God. Seven years he laboured. He fashioned her as though
Gladly forsaking all others she would live in sin on her own.
God took one look and hurried back up to Heaven.

Alf did nothing much after that. What I did up there, he said, will do.

# Dad's Wastwater

How bad was it, I ask myself, that day
The fear of not being rightly there
Of somehow being somewhere very far away
While you copied a famous man's painting of Wastwater
A distant beautiful lake you had never been to?

Well, I'll believe you were working close
All yourself concentrating on the thing that was not you
Eyes and hand steady and precise
Not thinking of anything but how to come near
That remote glacial beauty of rock and very deep water

Under a mild sky, copying, after the life elsewhere
How ill were you day after day
When you came back to it, to have another go
At getting what the proper artist got? Not so bad
I hear you say, those days I wasn't so bad

And from that far away bringing the cold lake home
Signed and dated (1989) and hung in the front room
I can almost hear you say it didn't
Look so bad after all, though I say it myself, as shouldn't
Quite good really, it looked, in a nice frame over the fire.

# As when

As when on a dull Sunday in Saint-Désir-le-Petit in the Café des Sports
(All our Sundays are dull, the dullest are terrifying)
We have been sitting three or four hours outside on the pavement smoking
And drinking slowly and the weather is neither hot nor cold
But dull, dampish, the skies unlikely to clear
And a nervousness spreads among us which nobody mentions
But we exchange remarks on nothing in particular
Till even that little is too much, we drink the glass off
And signal for another and light another fag
And as though we are all guilty, all ashamed
Look nobody in the eye but glance very furtively
Again and again up the road west or the road east
(Both are beautiful, both come in steeply on a hairpin)
And were we to be asked by an inquisitor of the conscience
Tell me honestly do you want the coming or do you not?
I'll bet you the drinks and cigarettes of a month of Sundays
No man could answer straight, Yes, I do or No, I don't
But all from under their brows in fear or in hope keep looking
West and east, like that, like that
As when on a usual dull Sunday into Saint-Désir-le-Petit
Suddenly and very fast like ten thousand kingfishers
Displacing the common air, the air we have fatigued by breathing it in and out
The sinuous long body, the draught, the whirr of them, the rush, the spate
So near, so undeniable, giving us never a glance
The riders pour, like that, oh like that!
As when out of the east or out of the west
At speed, racing to take with ease the steep curve away from here
Who for an instant were arriving
And for an instant were passing as close as I am now to you
(Their set faces, their purpose, sheer ability, the gift!)
Who for an instant then are leaving
And in the time that follows, the resuming Sunday
The church clock strikes another quarter or another hour
And we sit as we were and will till closing time
And no man asks his neighbour, Did you want that or did you not?

Are you glad of it or are you not? as when
The riders on another dull Sunday
Pass in ferocious glory under our noses
As we sit in the Café des Sports in Saint-Désir-le-Petit

# Open Mic

Sundays 3-7, the dead time
Is Open Mic here, twenty-five slots, in the dark side room
Where the piano stands and the posters
(Some big names) from way back hang and all the old guitars.

Few on in the first half stay till the interval
And few on in the second turn up before it
So there's never a crowd, never more than a handful
To be honest. In fact the last slot

Tends to entertain itself. True there's always
Two or three regulars at the bar
But by that time they'll be the worse for wear
And not paying attention. Bill himself does the intros:

And now, Ladies and Gentlemen, please welcome
The legendary, the one and only…
But while they're doing their best in the time allowed them
He'll be playing patience in his cubby hole. Me

I'm fond of Elaine. And now, says our compère
To tickle the ivories, a big hand for the lovely Elaine!
I could kill the bastard for that. His piano's never been
Even half in tune. I feel for her

How she bows so low over the keys, you'd say
She must be hearing something nobody else can hear.
I clap like mad, I don't care who knows. Last Sunday
A man from not round here blew in, he wore

A red cap and sat at the bar with a packet of crisps
And a pint of Bombardier. The show was nearly over
You'd have thought in all his born days he'd never seen anything like it
Got off his stool and moved in closer and closer.

And now, said Bill, last but very much not least
Put your hands together for Three for the Price of One
Fran ukulele, Carol, bless her, the vocals, Jimmy, the beast
Between two beauties, horn. It was Carol the stranger fixed on.

She sings with her eyes shut and over the years
Her voice has dropped a floor or two. That sound!
We had a vicar in once, he covered his ears.
She sang a Tom Waits number, 'Cold Cold Ground'

And then, with a smile: To cheer you up, here's one of my own.
The man in the red cap couldn't take his eyes off her
And when she'd done, he stood there quite alone
Crying, Bravo! Took his empty glass to the bar

Good night, he said to me. Then: 'lacrimae rerum'.
Brave name for a band that, said Carol when I told her.
Eh, Fran? Eh, Jimmy? Lacrimae Rerum!
Change our name and up our game? Whatever

Said Fran. You're the boss, Carol, said Jimmy.
Gone seven, the crowd were arriving.
Bill went back behind the bar where he belongs to be.
The serious drinking starts as the last Open Mic lot are leaving.

4

# Ballad of the barge from hell

A thousand miles off India
When nobody but God
Was watching them, 'Aye! Aye!', they said
And did as they were bid

And fed ten thousand tons of ash
To the fishes of the sea,
Fine as a dust of pollen
And gentle as mercy

And sailed away to somewhere else
And left a fading stain
That mizzled down among the fish
Soft as a small rain.

And now they'll drift for ever
For ever and a day
They drift and dream and watch and sleep
And none of them can say

Whether the dream is waking
Or whether the dream's asleep
They only know it's bad as hell
And wide and very deep

And they are blue with cold by day
Or white as bone with heat
And shine at nights like stinking fish
And taste in all they eat

An aftertaste of the mercury
And lead and cadmium
They sprinkled on the pretty fish
In God's aquarium.

# Ballad of the slave ship in the eye of heaven

A long way east of Africa
Above the innocent sea
Up nice and high in a hole in the sky
The Lord was taking tea
In blessed company.

Tell me, he said, what's that I hear,
That screaming sort of din.
Look down will you, and tell me, do –
I've lost my specs again –
What is that screaming din?

And one of the company looked down,
A general or an archbish:
It's the usual, from Liverpool,
Feeding your Worship's fish
A black and sickly dish

And the din you hear is the natural
Din of a thing like that,
The yes, the no, the to and the fro,
The feeders happy with it,
The food, however, not.

Is it good, the Lord asked a banker
Or a boss, that my captains toss
My black children, your kith and kin,
To my hungry fish? Some loss,
Said the banker or the boss,

Is natural and usual
In the divine economy
If with sugar and spice and all things nice
We're to bless the home country.
Ah, said the Lord, I see.

51

# Song: The way things are is the way things have to be

I get Park Lane and Mayfair
And you get the Old Kent Road
I get the Four Utilities
And you go to jail free
And the jail belongs to me
And that's just the way it is
So it is and it was always so
And I have another go.

If you ever come out of jail, friend
Take a stroll round my end of the board
Down Mayfair and Park Lane
And lift up your eyes to the rain
And give thanks unto the Lord
That you don't have the worry and the fret
Of property you can't let
Because the price isn't quite right yet.

You've nowhere to lay your head?
Remember what Our Saviour said:
Give to them who've already got
And from them that have nothing take that
Take the last little bit, take the lot.
And what else did the Good Lord say?
The poor aren't going away.
No the poor old poor are here to stay.

There's a bank error in my favour.
They're selling off the Old Kent Road
Next time I'm toddling round that end
I'll spend what I have to spend.
It's the least I can do for the town
Knock it down, sit tight on the site
Sit tight till the price is right.
There's a food bank opening near you.

In the game of life, my friend
Going round and round and no end
I've found that what most helped me
Is a sense of right and wrong
I learned it as I went along
I learned what's wrong by what's right.
In the game of Beggar Thy Neighbour
Right is when the price is right.

You are many, my friend, we are few
Oh indeed we are very very few!
And few as we are we get more and more
And there's less and less for you.
And now you're in jail again:
Well at least you're out of the rain.
It's my turn, I'll have another go
And another and another go.

# Ballad of the cruise ship

### 1

End game on, when the only news
Was the warming and rising of the seas
Said the Adviser, Best for you, I'm sure
Is you go on a cruise and never come ashore.
Absent yourselves, do as I advise
And you'll float on top much as before.

### 2

The *Hesperus*, big as Kensington,
Flew the colours of the Isle of Man
She had bars, gyms, casinos and eateries
And a hospital bigger than
Ten Amazon warehouses
And music without remission.

### 3

With their bouffant hair and their orange skin
And their dentures cast in a grin
The passengers looked the way you do
When you know yourselves to be the happy few
And the crew are not at all like you
And you don't know the tongue they whisper in.

### 4

Life everlasting will be yours on that ship
Said the Adviser. The poor are queuing up
To sell us any parts you might need
A spleen, a kidney, bollock, heart or hip
Place your order at the online shop
You'll be fitted next day, guaranteed.

**5**

East of Papua in an emptiness
The Captain, mortally troubled as he was
Hove to and let the good ship *Hesperus*
In silence join the outer ring
Of the congregated harm forever orbiting
A choke, a sort of blocked oceanic anus.

**6**

Observe, he said, this vast lethargic carousel
Its body-parts are indestructible
The law of their kind is they disassemble
After their fashion spawn and live the eternal
Death-in-life, smaller and smaller, more and more.
Tell me, is this a thought that you can bear?

**7**

Making south then under brazen skies
That hump, the Captain said, that mound ahead
Is our friend the blue whale and he is dead
And his shroud is gulls and flies
They know and they materialise
Whenever such a noble monster dies.

**8**

And somewhere in an archipelago
This also, said the Captain, you should know
What you see is what remains
Of a land of snowy mountain-tops and plains
Shall we pause and think of those below
Who managed pretty well not long ago?

**9**

Said Frank, You are not a lot of fun, mate.
We paid good money for an everlasting cruise
And don't want telling any time you choose
What you think we should know. I vote
We pack a picnic and launch the jolly-boat
And land and have a poke about.

**10**

Said the Adviser, That's the last thing I'd advise.
The savages, alas, did not all drown.
Most relocated up. They have sharp eyes.
They're watching. But the mutiny had grown.
The Captain shrugged. You'll get no crew. You're on your own.
I wash my hands of you. Say your goodbyes.

**11**

So thirteen fat old lads the worse for wear
While all the ranks of *Hesperus* raised a cheer
Pulled slowly (twirling like a leaf) towards the shore
While Frankie standing in the prow
A little tearfully remembered how
He'd rowed a girl called Pamela on a pond in – was it? – Slough.

**12**

Spying natives then, Ahoy! he bawled, We're white men
Trust us, we come in peace, we are good medicine!
Nearer and nearer, when the revolving jolly-boat
Brought red-faced Frank full on again
He got a poisoned arrow through his throat
And flopped and foamed and coughed his white teeth out.

**13**

Panic among his pals till they were clear.
Then seeing Frank was gone beyond repair
They photo'd him still frothing and sent forth
A hundred pics of him around the earth.
So many likes came back the larky shipmates swore
They'd deep-freeze Frank and crowd-fund his rebirth.

5

# I will hold you in the light

Between long absences having met again
Taking her leave she would say, I will hold you in the light
And has gone now where there's none.

So for the time allowed we shall hold her in our light.
More of the dark will come in if we let her go
And there's already too much of the dark where we are now.

Fit to be looked at, that is what one wants to be
Fit to be seen in the light of a friend's thinking.
And she always did have a look that enquired in a friendly fashion

How are you doing in the things that need to be done?
How've you been getting on with those things since I saw you last?
And asked to be looked at herself like that.

I remember watching my mother or her mother darn or sew
And that if I stood watching too close she would say to me
You are in my light, love, I can't see.

And remember also that if ever I came with a thing
Needing seeing to or putting right
Either one of the women would say, Bring it here, love, into the light.

Our dead, though their company grows, are not in our light.
We see better for them. And holding them in the light
See better what needs to be done or mended and how.

## First thing I saw then...

First thing I saw then was the windowed mirrored sun
In brightness, close, traversing our pale wall
So slowly that to measure its advance
You had to have looked away from it a while
Doing something else and then remembering
Glanced its way again. Such happiness
To see the far self-feeding self-consuming sun
Shaped by our window, cast by our looking-glass
Flowing across our bedroom wall
So indicating we are time well spent.

## Côté coeur

Already dying, she would lead the way to a table
Full in the window and watch out eagerly
Over the hurry of life under the sun, drank this
Till the coffees came, then woman to woman
Asked after my life that would continue a while yet
Beyond hers. The heart side, she asked,
What of the heart side, how is it for you nowadays
There? It is ten years ago, I turn away
And his hand feels over me so that my heart
Beats quietly with his pulse. All's well again. I will let myself
Go over into sleep and trust that the knot of vipers
Behind his forehead that bows into my hair
Will become like a gift of flowers when they settle from my hands
Into a sunny vase and all will be well again
A good long while. Often I see her
Turning from the haste of life on the daylit street
To enquire how things are for me nowadays
Heart side. Oh the friendly watching dead
How they must shake their heads over us in wonderment
That we make loveless even a minute of our time.

# The horseshoe

This horseshoe, lost by a workhorse in that ploughland
He trudged through in a fog towards Guillemont
The life-shape, the opening into, the putting out from
The footmark such as a spring makes on a hillside
This well-made useful iron thing, its finder, I
His younger daughter's elder son, have nailed it
Over our going out and our coming in
For luck, in honour of the forgiving earth
And in his memory who was strewn there with the iron
Brass, leather, flesh, blood and bone of many men.

# Fields

Ploughed, before sowing, one in the Cotswolds, the flints
Glinted and among them, dull, difficult to spot:
Small perfect lampshells, freed from the matrix, clean
And singular like the alive or dead today
At tidefall; sea-urchins, handy as slingstones
Their lovely petalling; many sharp belemnites.

Another under the olive trees at Gortys
In a breeze, in a watery dappling, the dry
Hard earth after the gush of poppies and thickly
Everywhere, easy to spot: four millennia
A stratum of sherds, warm krater handles, oh how
I wanted a girl's head lifted and the flute.

A third before Guillemont, ploughed, gently sloping
Quite without cover, in the deep chalk furrows
It was hard to walk, but the finds were evident:
A button, the shoe of a great shire horse, leather
Wire, iron, casings, lengths and splinters of bone
Eyes down, the stumbling men closer and closer.

# The tidebreak

*(for June and her three score years and ten)*

The tidebreak runs its course under enormous skies.
They view the western sea and the eastern uplands
And show foreknowledge of the unending lakes and mountains
In the opening largesse of the further and further North.

On the narrow tidebreak, ambling arm in arm, raised up only a little
But enough for a perspective of terra firma right
And the scant grass, brackish dubs and influx on your left
Under those skies, on either side, you have your belongings.

It's a trick of being human to love the immensities
That notice us no more than they did the long-lived race of trilobites.
The loudest voice will be drowned by an average high tide
But yours, so you and local, will run on softly in the time allowed

Telling stories of other quite peculiar folk. That farm over there
That spire, that railway line, once upon a time
When I was four or five... And we could tell by the taste
Whether it was land- or seaside the Christmas goose had browsed.

From the tidebreak you can point out where the dead used to live
And where they are gathered now. Nature abhors a frontier
And smiles at the bid to have all the good this side and all the bad that.
Drawing a firm line between the sea and the land

May help us feel a bit better among the uncertainties
But there's a murmur in us (like the tide, like the streams)
That does not love separations. The tidebreak is perfect to walk on
And talk about the dead. Right and left, above and forward

In so much space no wonder we clutch them close and look for home.
Walking the tidebreak together when the sea turns
We know it's a porous wall between us and our dead.
Where would we be without them? We'd be lost, we'd be nowhere.

# On the borderlands

Lately in the soft siesta red
On the borderlands I've lain
Watching a shadow-play on the screen

Of my shut lids, never commanding it
Unless one so attending
Draws like a quiet commanding

Pictures into the space. I've seen
A script, columns of a text I could not read
And did not grasp after and that may bide or fade

And come again or not. But better still
I've seen a stack of mountains and a path that knew
As I did not, the way it would go

To be in among them, climbing their many streams
And best in the contemplation are my ignorance
And faith, such patience

I think a good death may assume this shape and tone
On the borderlands, lingering
In the *locus amoenus*, life, watching

A play of pictures from the country of my heart
And there also inside
On the lids a script I may be able to read

Or, without coveting, watch it fade.

## Stele

One seated looking up at one who stands
These two across the gap are clasping hands
And seem, so carved, emergent from the stone
Or entering it. Millennia pass, and still one stands
Sorrowing over one who sits and still their hands
Are clasped as though the warmth of one
Could help the other going where there is none
And both are twain and both are all alone.
So in cold marble long beyond their lives
Look, love: finer than dust, feeling survives.

6

# Leaves

Of the leaves whose dying the sun had lit all afternoon
Come night, come sleeplessness, come fear of death
I made – no, I made nothing – I was shown
The fine gold particles of life in a mist, a small rain
And I knew that their slow fall would never end.

Whereupon I had some peace, my thinking stopped
And I lay only watching on the inner lids
Life precipitating very slowly and in silence
The leaves of life, the yellows, bronzes, reds
Shimmering a matt gold, the dots, the flecks.

Then this: the falls continuing shaped to an initial
Complex flowering majuscule – which one I could not tell –
And there at the heart of it in a clear space
Among the fronds, sat a young woman in white
Smiling, her hands calm in her lap. And that was all.

Behind and everywhere around her fell the motes of life.
The letter I couldn't make out began a missing script.
Love, will you will believe me this? I lay
As calm as she sat in her window, quietly
As the grains of life that were falling ceaselessly.

# Ash

There's an ash on Ingleborough, the lower bole
Looks like grey magma in a thick coil
As though it had boiled up and set and thereupon
Rose and spread, leafing and flowering
With every grace. And what's more

In a small cwm of her, a rowan has sprung up
Ash with another name. The men of Aran
Wadded their karst fields with a mix of sand
And seaweed in the brave hope of a potato crop
And lost it often, the crop and the soil

To the force-ten westerlies. But I'm sure if you
Climb to the Ingleborough ash in a year or so
Within her green you'll see a child wearing orange-reds
A mother raising her bird- or wind-borne daughter
Out of the grykes to the blue sky and all the while

Mining the limestone that was a warm sea once
For opportunities of sweet water
To get herself and her offspring a life under the sun
Down and down feeling her ways through
The packed mass graves of crinoids and brachiopods.

# Ways of being

When let, when annoying nobody's neighbour
How thoroughly and all in their own good time
They become what they had it in them to become
In the small buried talent. I saw one a week ago
It had ascended like smoke on a wind-still day

Slender, the tip of it feeling at the air
As delicately as an elephant's trunk. Walt Whitman
Thought he could turn and live with the animals
Who would not blather at him about his duty to God
And the chain-saw man next door. Myself

I'll seek acceptation among the trees. They do not
Run around all over the place snarling and bellowing
But stay still, moving in the fresh air. Another
I met that day, it reached out level and equally
On every side, in summer it would give you

A murmuring shade and the sight of yourself
Deep among the roots in a well shaft. It was of the kind
That cast themselves so abundantly over the earth
Scores of tractors and trailers lumbering down
Hard-rutted tracks from out of the deep province

Will mound a whole square high with colossal sacks
Of their light dry fragrance. The twinned helix
Is beautiful but for the naked eye the act itself appears
In ramification. You know by the blood-ways
On your own shut lids how thirsty life is underground.

# Sycamore

You feel the whole thing in the bid for it

The days of seed-cast must have been quite still
There's so much here not much can have gone down the wind

A tree coming into her own through years of room
Putting up, putting out, like a river
Ascending out of the waters under the earth
Feeling into finer and finer tributaries
Fingering the air
Already in April working up her progeny

And below, under the skirts, in the dappled shape of her
All the life above is being emulated
Testa, radicle, plumule
Till all the zone below is softly jostling
And the one is manifold
Each frail more-light-desiring cotyledon gapes
And through, across, comes a likeness in strengthening bronze
The idea of a tree is building
All the ground is prickling
Dense as a swarm, shoal, murmuration
As though every one in the gush of seed had taken
Every winged seed-head went home
And knows it wants to breathe

You see none of this on the urban concrete
And precious little in the parks and gardens
And this itself is only a visitant
Like a snowfall
It will disembody
It was an interlude, we were passing, we happened to witness it
Milt
Stardust
Fierce maledicted Lilith howling down the four winds
I have a forest in every seed of me…

# The blackthorn path

The blackthorn path had a before and after.
Coming from somewhere it went somewhere else
And was like every other path in those parts
As many in its branchings as the heart's
And brain's, and only for a while, a curving passage
Level and narrow did it become the blackthorn path
And tunnel the length of overarching thorn
Softened and quivering with sunny blossom.

I suppose you turned to see was I still following
I suppose I halted for the vision's sake:
The woman turning, smiling, her black hair
Amidst the blackthorn blossom. Not a photograph
Only the heart that stopped between two beats
Only the mind that still sees what was seen
Only this hand that scrawls a black-on-white
Tally of thanks across another sheet.

Yes, coming from somewhere it went somewhere else
And our brief stretch had drawn on many tributaries
And further along would split its riches further
And we were nowhere that was out of time
So when you turned to see me following
And when my eyes had printed you on the mind
And I stepped close what touched me deepest were
The snowflake-delicate petals in your hair.

# Plane tree

Everywhere its desire reached out and up
It had been hacked back and so, trunk and stumps
It stood nude, smooth, nacreous, blotched, ghastly
There on the street under the sun when the room's
New lovers pushed the windows open. Of this
Encounter what will live on in them is that
The tree from all over itself, from nowhere
Special, not from cuts, ends, not from places
Of precedent or encouragement but just
From wherever it could force into the light
Was leafing, flickering in small sprigs the way
Butterflies, still damp, blink for sun. It could not –
Not yet – run out the bunting of itself
Into its phantom limbs but it could and did
From pores all over, leaf. And this, on one
Another having learned to beckon up
Pleasure from anywhere on their nakedness
That latest pair on that small balcony
Facing that plane tree have not forgotten.

7

## My friend's belongings

In his mother tongues, or even in Turkish, Russian, Ukrainian
He would not struggle as he does in mine
After seven years here and far out of harm's way
To get across to me his lost belongings.
The tongues he is fluent in are the tongues of before.
English is after. He shows me the palms of his hands
As though what he had and held were still apparent there.
He has what we call an open face, he has tears in his eyes, he shrugs
And as though weighed down by what he cannot show me
His lifted hands fall back upon the table top.

On a good day he will search for the words on his phone:
Olive tree, fountain, racing pigeon.
And sometimes pictures. But as to pictures
I am wary since the bad day when without a word
He pushed into my sight and for ever into my head
What they did, laughing, in his country, to a twelve-year-old.
Such things lodge now in the top stratum of his belongings.
He wakes sweating and screaming out of the old nightmares
And feels in the darkness for his phone
Which faithfully supplies him with stuff from home, for the new.

How he struggles to excavate his buried treasures!
In my mother tongue he cannot find the words
But I know, on good days, that he wants to prove to me
Back then his circumstances were very different.
And I do believe that he cultivated his garden
Launched beautiful canny pigeons into the clear skies
Was hospitable to friends and the stranger at the door
And what God put into his hands
Far more than a tithe of it he passed on to the needy.
He calls me brother, he does not begrudge me my belongings.

# Young woman with a cello on the metro

In the crowded carriage I was given a space of time
To look at her for whom the doors had slid
Open and she stepped in with the cello on her back
Bright white, almost doubling her, unslung it, stood
Barely a yard from me who stood admiring her
For the allotted stops until, entering the dark
Before the last, becoming visible in the window glass
Quickly she withdrew a long and ornate silver pin
From her black hair and while the mirror lasted
Shaped up that tumble to her satisfaction
And speared it fast. I watched. The station came
She slung the cello on, the doors slid open for her
And out she stepped, into the lights, the crowd
Into the city with her hair just as she wanted it
And all her music carrying on her back.

## Old men walking the streets

These muttering old men in the red headgear
I feel for them, I think they go on living with the certainty
It won't ever be delivered now what fifty years ago they believed
They were in at the making of, I suppose

They go back to unheated rooms in places not their own
And make a bit of tea and contemplate
Their empty hands, these lost old men
All day traipsing the disappointed streets

And always alone though my observations convince me
Even in this small town they are many
In their caps and bonnets which are so startlingly red
Above the grizzled face and the faded light of their eyes.

# Unborn child of Elizabeth Gaunt

Losing her child (they beat it out of her)
She lived, her name is written in the stone
Among the other named, the dead eighteen
And her lost child without a name is with her there.

The sabred, trampled, bayoneted, shot are dead.
Unborn is different. Elizabeth's child evicted
By lawful fists and truncheons before her time
Having no life, always unborn, given no name

That child, that day of the banners and the bands
The Wakes of Justice when the generations flowed
Into the city from the towns and the black uplands
That child carried in secret in a multitude

May she not still be called a faith in hiding
Halted for now, leaving the loss, the space
Herself a power and a promise biding
For a mother and a local dwelling place?

Truly you have passed on a faith to keep:
Still wanting the birthright you were dying for
(A country fit to live in), to believe somewhere
Local the lost child bides whose name is Hope.

# Young woman asleep

Another for want of footfall
Closed – what was it ever? I can't remember – but now
At least its doorway has become a kip
And she's out of the drizzle and in the dismal daylight

There she sleeps and of her shows
From among the damp blankets and her few belongings
Only her face
Quiet as a child. As the peppered moth

Evolved to become invisible
On the satanic bark of northern trees so she
For survival closes her eyes and assumes
The pale still countenance of an angel

And sleeps the innocent sleep in the public view because
In broad daylight no jovial young men
Will break from the midst of their fellow citizens
And unzip themselves and piss all over her.

She is safe, her fellow humans are mostly very busy
And if they glance her way as they hurry on by
She has come to trust
That her achieved appearance of being wholly at their mercy

Will remind them there are things they must never do
And in this faith
She sleeps the few hours of a winter afternoon
For all the world like a child with loving parents in a house and home.

# Rescue dog

There's a ghost of childishness in the grown size of him –
The way he lifts up his eyes through the fringe of a mop of hair.
She embroidered the coat he wears. She knows
As he cannot, the cost of their understanding.

He has learned her face, the tones of voice
In which she speaks to him, her hands helping or fondling
But above all he has got by heart her face
From where his trust comes. He knows what he owes her

But not what she will pay. Boarding the bus, she says
To nobody in particular, His back legs are going
Ten years he was on the streets and only
Two has he been with me. They rode one stop.

He couldn't have walked that far. She helps
His weight down onto the concrete. No life for a dog
She says, the streets. Two short years I've had him and already
His back legs are going. But what can you do?

# The Marazion man

Waking I thought of the Marazion man
Who for the twelvemonth in all weathers
Took a camp chair to her grave and sat there
Telling her about his day. The long days were easiest
For then he need not visit till the promise of dusk
And perhaps by that time he had gone out with the starlings
To the North Coast and only set off home
To the South when they did. Those nights he slept.
He made sure to fix with her the hour of their conversation
And kept to it. He didn't want her worrying.
All the things were to say that had always been to say
And more, more that he could not bear she did not know
Till he told her. Hence his rush of words.
The short days were the worst. He thought it indecent
To haunt the common acre during the hours of darkness
And they were many and each one very long.
In daylight he was familiar, nobody accosted him.
He sat on his folding chair and told her his day
While the sun went down into the western sea.
Everyone in that place had a purpose
And how they managed was their own affair.
It is half a lifetime ago already.
The tombs have extended into the lower plots
Small decent necropolis growing in its own good time.
I shouldn't be able to find their stone among so many
But this morning I saw him alone out on the perimeter
Before there was a stone, while the earth was settling over her
And on his camp chair he was singular
Leaning forward, leaning down a little
Telling her his news, biding for hers.

# Dancer

This five-year-old dancing to the music of a man
Who died a long long time ago, when I tell her
She is very graceful she nods as though to say
You don't need to tell me that, and goes on dancing

Not knowing and nor would it interest her to learn
What kind of grace I'm telling her she has. For it isn't
That of the music nor a matter of whether
She keeps time or not. The man who made the music

And died too young was a child to the bitter end
And I think he'd have loved almost as much as I do
The way her right sock will keep coming down and how
Pulling it up again, she jigs on her left foot

Without a smile. Her grace is a serious matter
But as if through the eyes of the old mask, through aeons of tears
Broke such jolly tunes the celestial bodies
Skipped and skated. Her time's not exactly his but nor

Does she use his music merely for her back-cloth
It's more a place and her way of being in that place
Free to keep what time she likes. So I think Lilith
Danced in Eden and the flames and waters of the earth

The trees, the stones and all kinds of other living things
In a solemn gaiety danced their own dances
With her. And it's true, child, you don't need me telling you
You're graceful. The words, words, words: you're lighter without them.

# Mazey

Glory! Glory! Glory! Here comes one who abhors inertia!

Two months arrived on the hurtling planet Earth
Weighing barely a pound with a soft plump belly and claws
Unsheathing out of softness that are as savage as fish-hooks and a spine
Sharp as a picked fish's, here she comes now, a godsend, the heart pitty-pat.

Objects lying still, you amaze her. Can you not glide, leap, fly?
And – this is innocence, this is life dropping among you
Wide-eyed and without prejudice – she will chivvy not just the likely
The floating golden ribbon, the ping-pong ball – but you also
The very unlikely, you there, clothes peg, you there
Yoghurt pot lid, and even you, dry old crust, this child will clout you
Into what you did not know you had it in you even to desire:
Movement. She will call forth
The tune of one and all of you, your feeling for surfaces, what
You sound like skittering across or, flung up, crash-landing on. One and all
You amaze her and does that not deserve your thanks? Dance then
Do the best you can, egg her on, for she did not cuff you into life
To watch the performance, she is of it, in it, heart and soul in the joined
            game itself
And what she asks of you is that you raise your game and hers.

Then off she strolls, and leaves you to the quiet life.

I feel for Ping-pong kicked into touch over there
I suppose him to be harbouring the memory of movement
And in the memory the want. Creature, come back
Jump-start me again, bat me from paw to paw across the floor
Throw me up so I bounce and resound on the sunny kitchen tiles.
I did not waste your time. What you made me do was in me to do
And lives there still. Sleep if you must but dream of fun and waking
Turn your greeny-yellow eyes my way.

# English lesson

Life, Constantine, he said. And held up his right hand
As if there on the palm within a clutch of fingers
He showed the life of the stanza, paragraph or scene
That we were being asked to understand

And he would offer it one or other of us
To take a close look at before it blew
From the calyx of his hand into the air
And that it could not be contained we must grasp too.

Of course, behind his back we took the piss:
Life, Sandiford... Life, Horrocks... Life, you, you and you...
Lifting our paws, donning the mask of rapture
Swapping a handful, Here, try some of this.

What lines, what sentences, I don't remember now
So many, countless many I think they were
He read with us and raised the life they harboured high
A breath of life, a passage, and let it fly.

I woke last night and lay a good while there
Lay in the dark and saw that conjuror
Scoop up a little life and offer a glimpse of it to me
I saw the sunlight in a dusty room, I saw

Motes dancing. Life, Constantine, he said.
I see it, sir, I see the words that live
I see you giving us what you had to give
And thank you who still teach me from the dead.

# I watched a man...

I watched a man letting the ferry go.
I leaned in the stern at ease, he stood below
In a stranger's clothing on the concrete quay
With his foolish suitcase for anyone to see
His mortal trouble. How I love arriving
At an island within ten minutes I'll be leaving
And will not see again! I love a ferry
That gets the off and on done in a hurry.
And there he stood, my man, in that pell-mell
Averted with only the one thought in his skull.
On shore they let the great ropes slacken and drop
On deck the winches hauled and coiled them up
And still he faced away and still he could not see
Love anywhere on that vacated quay.
Behind his back we slipped from him, so fast
Departure is, so soon across the gap he lost
Significance. No doubt he raised
His eyes beyond the quay and beyond the town
To where on rock under the sun and moon
Unwanted things begun were once exposed.

# The morning after

### 1

This morning, friend, your courtesy alarms me.
I think you think I am in need of it.
Another man's honeysuckle overhangs the pavement:
You halt and beckon me through under the scent.
You smile, I smile. As I go on my way and have you behind me
I am almost certain that you bowed.
What is it, friend, fellow-citizen?
I am almost certain you will never be my enemy
But your manners this ordinary morning have alarmed me.
Is there something I should know and do not know?
Like you, I am a family man
Is the Law still my defender as it is yours?

### 2

Nothing personal, neighbour, but if I don't tell you
Somebody else will. Today isn't yesterday. Talking loudly
Won't do you any favours. It has become obvious
You're not our shade, are you? There are people
(Not me) will tell you your headgear
Is out of place. I know one lady
She'll tell you to your face when she uses public transport
She just wants to be with her own kind, thank you very much.
And my own father, God rest his soul
I can hear him saying he didn't round up the Mau Mau
To see the country overrun like this. Nothing personal, neighbour
I can hear him giving you his opinion
That only people born here belong here and by born here
He means way back. Don't mind me asking, neighbour
Where do you call home?

# Carousel

November, early dark, and in the drizzle
On wasteland strung with lights: the fair
And at the heart of it, in all the glare and roar
The tuneful measured anticlockwise-turning carousel

Watchers encircling it. Here is a space
To play at letting go, to try, having come thus far
How many seconds separation you can bear
After the desert and the sea, after the ice

The hungering, the deaths and too much entering through
The eyes into the kitty of bad dreams, at last
They bid in this arena for another lease of trust
And watch their kids go half a revolution out of view

One sailing solo on a swan and then
Two clutching tight on an elephant arrive
And leave and you can see they do not quite believe
The looping tune will bring them back again

To grown-ups so long at the world's mercy
Without a tongue to plead who stand now silent in a ring
And watch their flesh and blood within it orbiting
And wager all on a quaint machinery

And entertain the idea that in this pleasure ground
Playing at severance is permissible
And that the ancient music is reliable
And keeping time against the clock will bring the children round

Take and return the elephant and the swan
Strew lost and found on that discouraged audience until
They will believe it if the children will:
You let us out of sight and, look, we come again!

This travelling Babel, here three nights allowed
To set up shop on out-of-town terrain
Blessed be the flare of it, blessed be the soft rain
So both the circles, those who stand and watch and those who ride

The friendly animals in a fairy tale
At every revolution on the fabulous flat earth
May see through rain and tears beloved faces lit with mirth
Haloed, here and now, and real.

# 8

## SIX MORE HÖLDERLIN FRAGMENTS

## 1

*Singing of the Muses at midday*

When Pan sleeps and there is a fearful stillness. If you could begin
to imagine such a state your dawning sense would be of an ever-
lasting time in a place without borders. He sleeps very lightly. Any
creature speaking, especially any human, would wake him. No wind
stirs, so nor does any leaf or grass. The springs, the streams? They
move as they will and are audible. Indeed, some in the darkness
under the earth *become* faintly audible in the stillness when Pan is
sleeping. Fearful stillness, he must not be woken. And it was then,
in the stillness, in the trembling heat of midday, that the Muses
sang, the Nine, a nine-part complex singing to the music of the
springs and streams that live and move and have their being in
the sunlight and in the darkness.

In his sleep, Pan listens. And the rest of life also, at that hour, in
that heat, in that stillness, listened deeply to the Muses singing,
they quietened their breathing and all their manifold ways of life
into a sort of hibernation, they transformed themselves into an
attentive silence, all had a part in the making of that silence. How
they listened! And they heard the singing of the Muses, the nine
intricately joining, parting and reuniting voices, the harmony
through which the springs and streams of living water threaded.

Pan's anger if woken is terrible. He gives a shout that rises to the
heavens and reverberates round a hemisphere. For he loves the
singing of the Muses and cannot abide the loss of it. And the rest
of life too, all its species, even including (back then) the humans,
they feared Pan's shout of anger if they woke him, but more they
feared the loss of the singing of the Muses in the stillness in the
midday heat.

**2**

*But soon my voice*
*Will go about like a dog in the heat of the day*
*In the lanes behind gardens where people live*

Thirsting, and nobody heeding it, the voice goes about like a stray dog, crying, Why do you not thirst as I do in this day and age? The gardens are well tended and well watered. Their owners sit at ease in privacy, they take pleasure in the plashing of fountains, the scents of familiar flowers, the singing of familiar birds. They congratulate themselves on the beauties they command. And crying, Why do you not thirst as I do? the voice runs hither and thither between the gardens down the lanes and out into the deserted public square and howls, howls there in the noon-day heat and returns again and again into the maze of walled gardens where people live at ease and do not thirst.

**3**

*the windows of heaven being opened*
*And the night spirit unleashed,*
*The stormer of heaven who has swayed our land*
*With tongues, many and ungovernable,*
*And shunted*
*Rubble till now*

In our understanding the windows of heaven are not opened but smashed and through them are flung, headfirst with their wings cut off, the angels. Night herself is beautiful, of course, and the night spirit is her coming over all five senses and into the living souls of happy people, lovers, for example. So she was but she is dead now with every good thing else and in our present understanding the night spirit and the ransacker of heaven are one and the same, namely Evil, who has unleashed another Babel on our land so that nobody understands nor tries to understand the tongue of anybody else. We house in rubble and are killed and buried in rubble. And the best hope now for our once lovely city with its slender white towers and bridges, its busy bright markets and all its jasmine gardens and marble fountains, must be in the distant future to become an involuntary park, as other sites have, and be allowed to flourish in joyful relief that we have gone and will not come again.

# 4

*We also once were glad*
*In the early morning when the works were still*
*On a holiday and the flowers also in that stillness*
*For certain bloomed more beautifully and the living waters sprang forth*
  *brightly*

Far away and seven years later he would remember the life that had been his in his own country when he was a useful man, a pharmacist, and people came to him for help and if they could not afford the medicines he did not charge. He would tell this not to praise himself but to indicate his happiness then and his good fortune. What God gave me I gave much of it to others, he said, and was given more, and more I gave. On a rest day or a holiday how glad he was in those days among his flowers in peace and quiet and the fountains of the living waters endlessly, so it seemed, replenishing. Quiet on a sabbath or the day of a festival there among family and dear friends he rejoiced in his happiness because out of it, like the fountains, he would give and give.

**5**

*And so with drops*
*He stilled the sighing of the light that was like*
*A thirsty beast in those days when around Syria*
*The homely grace of the butchered infants wailed*
*In dying*

As a grown man, soon to die, he has it on his conscience that at his birth they butchered thousands when the only child they really wanted dead was him. The light, witnessing it, has thirsted ever since, and his few drops, teardrops, drops of blood, do nothing to assuage the parched lands. No wonder any harm done to children was another dagger in his heart, no wonder he kneeled and opened his arms to them. Homely, local, their grace. And every home from which they were taken, every neighbourhood, thirsts for ever in the absence of their grace. Doubtless there were slaughters of innocents before we began again with the numbering of the years, but the slaughter in Syria, in what would come to be called the Holy Land, that is ours, our sign, the birthmark on our foreheads. That was the Fall, not Eve's smile and her teethmark in the apple. Sighing of the light, a thirst beyond assuaging. And a rabid beast, *homo lupus*, lives up to his modern beginnings.

**6**

*When in the olive country and*
*Somewhere sweetly foreign*
*Fountains along grassy ways*
*The trees unknowing in the desert*
*The sun stabs*
*And the heart of the earth*
*Lifts up where round*
*The hill of oaks*
*Out of a burning land*
*The rivers and where*
*On Sundays amid dancing*
*The thresholds are hospitable*

As if a family carrying all they could and pushing a grandfather, curled like an ancient burial, and sometimes an exhausted toddler with him, in a handcart, came not to hell but by fabulous good fortune to somewhere sweetly foreign where the olive is cultivated and there are gracious fountains every mile or so along ways that are grassy and easier on the feet... As if they had come, three generations of them, from a house and home in a burning land and across a parched expanse where occasional trees stood in ignorance and innocence and they rested under them as long as they dared and rose and set off again dead beat and thanked their lucky stars that the heavens were empty... And as if at last they came to a river and the river parted like an embrace around a notable hill that was crowned with oaks and the warm heart of the earth opened to them, the travellers, the foreigners, and they found they had hit upon a Sunday or a holiday, the day of a local festival, there was music and the streets of the village were slung with blossom and they walked in silence, not yet trusting, and men and women and children stood in the open doors and greeted them, saying, Welcome, strangers...

9

# Chorus from Sophocles' *Oedipus at Colonus*

Famous for horses, nowhere was
More beautiful on earth
Than this place you have come to, stranger
Bright Colonus, here
The many nightingales sang loud and long
Amid deep greenery and under the wine-dark
Berried ivy, down
The untrodden ways that no storms shook
Nor fierce sun burned
The god came, Dionysus came
For revelry
With the undying
The ever-fostering nymphs.

Here in the dew of heaven
Day upon day narcissi used to thrive
Whose clustering beauty
The goddesses had always worn for crowns
With the golden shining crocuses and never
Did the unsleeping streams
Of Cephissus dwindle but they roamed
For pasture and every day
With undefiled waters
Over the swelling land
Gave easy birth. I tell you, stranger
The Muses loved to dance here and the golden-
Reined Aphrodite rode...

# Chorus from Sophocles' *Antigone*

Monstrous, a lot. But nothing
So monstrous as man. For he
Unkind to his own kind
Inducting them young into dealing and war
Dying, bequeathing
Them the developing curse
Of his enterprise, on the earth, on the seas
And into the air
He visits himself
At best in folly
But often with malice aforethought. Man
The wrong turning
Who ordered the fire of the sun
Into the streets, the parks and the schools of a town
And there in broad daylight
Cast people as lasting shadows, for him
On whose brow is inscribed, Beware
There is nothing I will not do
Why now should the warm-blooded dolphin
The smiling, the playful, the dancer, the maker of music
Who ferried the singer Arion to safety, why now
Should this friend intercede?

Oh man the killer
Who multiplies
Who schemes in his sleep after ways of living for ever
Who smothered the law in his heart
In these days of the melting poles
Of earthquake and flood and the cavalry charge of the tides
He knows it now
The law
By virtue of having transgressed and will stand
On the shore as the leaden waves
For his comfort deliver him
Carrion

Starfish and whales. Oh swiftly climbing and fouling
The lovely curve of the sky
The infinite swarm of death
Will fall on his fields
And he will have nothing to answer
The child who asks who are they
Passing on the last of the light? They are
Persephone in rags
Leading her blinded mother by the hand
Seeking an entrance to preferable Hades.

# Dolphin

She flung up here on the dirty tideline, those
Are bloody holes that were her eyes
And that encrusted spattering of white is where
The gulls perched hacking at them and the rest of her.

Another subtracted from the cheerful company
Of creatures who seemed once to love humanity
And surfaced, smiling, snorting, leaped and played
Around our prows that once were dolphin-eyed.

With them, warm blood in common, we had access
To the ancient depths. The loss, the loss!
She lies now stranded under the sun and moon
Eyeless, ripped to the bone, not fit to be seen

Among our trash that will live for ever.
Come soon, spring tide, recover what's left of her.

# NOTES

### The lucky and the unlucky (29)

The poem comes from beachcombing in Scilly. At very low water, looking for nothing in particular, I found a Roman coin: Faustina, wife of Marcus Aurelius, on one side, Diana Lucifera ['bearer of light'] on the other. Then I met the coastguards, looking for the body of a young man, a swimmer, who had drowned. The *Grace* is a lifeboat, the *Emerald Dawn* a local fishing boat.

### Unborn child of Elizabeth Gaunt (80)

The title is an inscription on the Peterloo monument in Manchester.

### Six more Hölderlin Fragments (91)

These continue the sequence of seven in *Elder* (2014). My note then will serve again here:

> I modelled these 'Hölderlin Fragments' on Hölderlin's own 'Pindar-Fragmente' which he composed in 1803 at the time of his beautifully strange versions of Sophocles' *Oedipus* and *Antigone*. Each of the nine texts consists of a fragment of Pindar's verse, closely translated into Hölderlin's own late language, and a passage of prose set below it as though to explain and comment. But that comforting relationship – text + exegesis – is belied by the practice. Out of the fragment of a poem, elusive in its peculiar beauty, Hölderlin derived a poetic prose which itself reads like translation from a strange elsewhere and itself seems to call for exegesis. The whole sense of each piece is generated in the interplay of ancient text and modern reading. Resisting exegesis, they reach out from the borders of his alienation for future readers to continue them.

See also my Friedrich Hölderlin, *Selected Poetry* (Bloodaxe Books, 2018), pp. 240-46.

### Choruses from Sophocles' *Oedipus at Colonus* and *Antigone* (98)

These are further versions, in the light of the worsening climate emergency, of those I did some years ago which appear on p. 231 and pp. 332-3 of my Friedrich Hölderlin, *Selected Poetry* (Bloodaxe Books, 2018).

### Dolphin (101)

This is a 'translation' into our modernity of a poem by the Ancient Greek poet Anyte of Tegea. She was writing in the early 3rd century BC.